Ireland, 1588

Wreck of the
Spanish Armada

Michael Sheane

A.H. STOCKWELL
PUBLISHERS SINCE 1898

Published in 2023 by
Michael Sheane
in association with
Arthur H Stockwell Ltd
West Wing Studios
Unit 166, The Mall
Luton, Bedfordshire
ahstockwell.co.uk

Contents

Also from Michael Sheane

Ulster & Its Future After the Troubles (1977)
Ulster & The German Solution (1978)
Ulster & The British Connection (1979)
Ulster & The Lords of the North (1980)
Ulster & The Middle Ages (1982)
Ulster & St Patrick (1984)
The Twilight Pagans (1990)
Enemy of England (1991)
The Great Siege (2002)
Ulster in the Age of Saint Comgall of Bangor (2004)
Ulster Blood (2005)
King William's Victory (2006)
Ulster Stock (2007)
Famine in the Land of Ulster (2008)
Pre-Christian Ulster (2009)
The Glens of Antrim (2010)
Ulster Women – A Short History (2010)
The Invasion of Ulster (2010)
Ulster in the Viking Age (2011)
Ulster in the Eighteenth Century (2011)
Ulster in the History of Ireland (2012)
Rathlin Island (2013)
Saint Patrick's Missionary Journeys in Ireland (2015)
The Story of Carrickfergus (2015)
Ireland's Holy Places (2016)
The Conqueror of the North (2017)
The Story of Holywell Hospital: A Country Asylum (2018)
Patrick: A Saint for All Seasons (2019)
The Picts: The Painted People (2019)
Pictland: The Conversion to Christianity of a Pagan Race (2020)
Irish & Scottish Dalriada (2020)
The Roman Empire (2021)
The Ancient Picts of the Scottish Highlands of the Seventh Century (2021)
The Celtic Supernatural (2022)
Grace O'Malley (2023)

Ireland, 1588

When the Sea Gave Up Its Dead

Nearly every schoolboy knows that 1588 is the date of the Spanish Armada, when the Spanish fleet sailed from Lisbon to England with the aim of overthrowing Elizabeth I and reinstating Catholicism; this was never their destiny however, and more than five thousand soldiers perished in the fierce winds and waves around Britain and Ireland. In retreat, the Armada sailed into the North Sea, sailed back around the north coast of Scotland, and then south west towards Ireland. The ships were within sight of Benbulben and the Dartry Mountains on the coast of County Sligo. Three great galleons of the Armada wanted to take shelter from the storms. One of the ships, the *San Juan de Sicilia*, had a crew of 343 men; another ship, *La Lavia*, had a complement of 274 men and the third ship was similarly overcrowded.

For four days the ships swung at their anchorage, and without any small boats, the Spaniards could not transfer much-needed food from the mainland. The three forlorn ships were bathed in the Irish sunset, their crew on the lookout for reefs – yet they were cast upon the rugged shore, and strong waves wrought gaps in the hulls of all three.

Hundreds of men died in an instant; those that escaped were slain by the loyal Gaels and by the army of Queen Elizabeth, all of whom were relieved that the Armada had been driven by the winds around the east and north coast of Britain, with over one thousand dead bodies washing up on her shores. In Ireland, a handful of the Spanish were able to receive help from local clans who bore no allegiance to the Tudor regime, but nevertheless many bodies were washed up over a two-mile stretch of the coast line: Atreeda

Strand was known henceforth as *Carraig na Spáinneach*, in English 'Spaniard's Rock'.

A map drawn in 1609 carries an inscription telling us that three Spanish ships were wrecked off Dernish Island in 1588; many other vessels were also wrecked in Munster, from Galway to Killala Bay, and in both County Sligo and Ulster.

The names of some of these ill-fated vessels are known whilst others can only be guessed. Those men that managed to survive shipwrecks were in many cases hanged or put to the sword. Some of the surviving Spaniards sought mercy from the local natives – looking to surrender to the Gaels and the English – but were butchered and hunted like animals, killed upon their capture. One group of survivors were kept in confinement for several days but then butchered rather than handed over. In Mayo, Galway, Clare and Kerry the Gaels gave no aid to the Spanish as they were fearful of their English overlords. An English official recorded that 5,600 Spaniards had drowned, with only one thousand being recorded as having escaped from their wrecked transports.

The number of ships that managed to make it back to Spain is not known for sure. However, all along the Ireland's north-west and south-west coast are locations known to locals as *Spanish Rock* or *Spanish Point*; grimly, there are also those places named *Spaniards' Grave* in memory of the tragedy as well as man's inhumanity in an age when there was much cruelty.

Fear Was the Key

The Spaniards were easily outnumbered by the native Irish, who watched the storm-battered galleons seek anchorage on their coast. On board, food was running out and there was no water left in the barrels; all they had was beer. The Gaels had learnt that the Spaniards were in the English Channel and that Queen Elizabeth feared for her throne. This was an age when news travelled slowly, and if the Spaniards were able to land on the coast of England, the life of an Englishman would not be worth living.

The Spanish galleons were large and sported heavy guns. Their decks carried many well-trained soldiers who were said to be the best fighters in all of Europe. If the Spaniards were able to come ashore in England, then Ireland would be ablaze with insurrection. Neither the Gaels nor the English had enough prisons to hold all those captured; regardless, there was no way they could feed such a high number of prisoners, thus starvation was inevitable. There were not even enough soldiers to provide escort for captured Spanish prisoners and so the order was given to execute all those detained.

Prior to the Armada setting sail, all men were paid their due wages. Many of the nobility were lavishly dressed in fine clothes and sporting velvet cloaks. There was a ship called the *Gran Grin*, a large merchant vessel of some 1,160 tons, commanded by Don Pedro de Mendoza and having a complement of 329 soldiers and sailors. The vessel was leaking badly and the crew were using buckets to get rid of the water. They saw the island of Achill with its soaring mountain; many of the men landed on the island only to be attacked by the natives. The ship itself continued to drift, so the sixteen men that had remained on board also ventured ashore. They too were captured and handed over to the Governor of Connaught. The Spaniards had planned to capture the currachs[1] of the English and the Gaels. Achill was not unique with regard to these happenings; a near identical situation was taking place on nearby Clare Island. The Governor of Achill passed on to the English information regarding the plight of the Spaniards, also noting that if the Gaels attacked, it would drive a wedge between two Catholic powers.

---

1. A type of Irish boat with a wooden frame over which animal skins or hides were stretched.

Dangerous Years

Queen Elizabeth's secretary of state was Sir Francis Walsingham and the present condition of Ireland was but one of his worries, for the Gaels were addicted to papistry, change of government and licentious liberty. It had become known that they were sympathetic towards the Spanish and so Sir William Herbert, an influential nobleman of some culture, suggested ways of placating the Irish rather than the use of force. Walsingham paid a great deal of attention to these suggestions, as well as to the many reports about the threats there existed to the English.

In January 1586, Sir John Perrot – Elizabeth's Lord Deputy in Ireland – was becoming nervous, for it had been reported by the English Secret Service under Walsingham that Spain was preparing to invade England, and it was rumoured that some twenty thousand soldiers would land in Ireland. As 1586 faded into 1587, Walsingham's reports to London became more intense; it was now a fact that Phillip of Spain was massing his forces in Lisbon; the English prayed to God that the Catholic forces would be defeated before setting sail.

At this time, bitter feuds divided many of the Irish Clans – especially those in the south of the country. The natives were more concerned about obtaining personal power than forming a united front against England. Ireland's geography was also vastly different from how it is today; the land was swampy and un-drained, with small patches cleared to grow corn, and brushwood covering much of its surface. Only within the Pale – that part of Ireland directly under the control of the English government – was there a semblance of a food system. Before the Spaniards arrived in Ireland, local

5

uprisings had been suppressed. In Limerick, Cork and Waterford counties, the Desmond overlordship dated back to Norman times. The sixteenth century Earl of Desmond was no fighter himself, but his cousin James FitzMaurice FitzGerald dreamed the old dream of banishing the English from his country with assistance from foreign aid. Thousands died in Munster as the rising got underway, the province becoming a wasteland. Reports sent back to England told how Munster had been ravaged, herds of cattle had been lost, the earth had not been tilled and that now, famine stalked the land. An English gentleman writing from Cork recorded the fact that in his neighbourhood some thirty thousand souls had perished from hunger in a period of just six months. Edmund Spencer, the Elizabethan poet who was one of the government's planters, described Munster thus:

> ...Out of every corner of the woods and glynnes they came creeping forth upon their hands, for their legges could not beare them; they looked like anatomies of death; they spake like ghosts crying out of their graves; they did eate the dead carrions, happy where they could finde them, yea, and one another soon after, insomuch as the very carcasses they spared not to scrape out of their graves; and if they found a plot of watercresses or shamrocks, there they flocked as to a feast for the time; that in short space of time there were none almost left, and a most populous and plentifull countrey suddainely left voide of man and beast

Lord Grey, who had directed the blood-stained repression of the uprising, was recalled to London. He was out of favour with Elizabeth and her government despite having mostly restored law and order; it was the justice of some of his actions that were criticised, including the massacre at the Siege of Smerwick and the hanging of the former Chief Justice Nicholas Nugent on no more than a vague suggestion of complicity in the Desmond rebellion.

The King of Spain

Long before the Armada incident, it seemed inevitable that England and Spain would come to be at war, because in the sixteenth century, Spain was enormously powerful. Her men were well-trained and disciplined, and King Philip of Spain – a careful and prudent man – had a firm grip on his empire, something England did not. For a long time Philip had his eye on South America, where he later established Spanish power in the way of colonies. Elizabeth had been excommunicated by the Pope for furthering her father's Protestant stance, and Catholic Europe would now unite against her at the Pope's bidding. The Armada was an example of how both religious and trading interests could be intertwined within the context of war.

As Philip pondered in his chamber in the centre of El Escorial, he received news that Sir Francis Drake was preparing to fight the Spaniards... after he had finished his game of bowls. Drake was a legendary figure of great magnitude in the history and traditions of England. He was the son of a Puritan, a splendid seaman and a daring adventurer.

Philip was fully aware of Drake's capabilities. In the summer of 1572 Drake had sailed to Panama – this was the isthmus from which Philip mined the gold in Peru. The Spaniards had subdued the native Incas with only a small number of troops. Drake and his armed company landed south of the Chagres river and raided the mule trains which were loaded with precious stones and silver bars. The bars were too heavy to carry, so Drake buried them in a secret place – and even today, people seek out the burial place as Drake never returned to recover them. He then captured a Spanish galleon that had sailed from Lima containing a year's worth of mining;

there were twenty tons of silver bullion, thirteen chests of silver and a hundredweight of gold.

In 1585 he set out again for the West Indies with a force of 2,500 men in twenty-five privateer vessels. Though the ships did not sail under the Jolly Roger, there was little doubt that many today would adjudge them as pirates. The force had been patronised by Elizabeth and society's wealthiest men, some of whom were members of the Privy Council.

Drake began by raiding the town of Vigo, where he robbed the local church of its valuables. His fleet then sailed to the Cape Verde islands, where the town was razed to the ground. At Saint Domingo in the West Indies he burned down half of the town and agreed not to raze the other only if he received a payment of twenty-five thousand ducats, his price for sparing the inhabitants. At Cartagena he extorted thirty thousand ducats in the same way, and then returned to England, circumnavigating the globe with the holds of his fleet laden with treasure. The shareholders who invested in his adventure were delighted with their return. In Spain there was much prosperity too, because Peru had been stripped of its gold and silver.

In the eyes of Philip, the attack on his ships was an act of war. He at once saw the danger: the Spanish empire would cease to exist if its overseas interests were plundered by the English.

Philip now made his decision to invade England and remove Elizabeth.

The Fate of the Armada

In Spain, shipwrights swarmed over small and large ships to construct the invading Armada. Philip was convinced that he should start work immediately and keep the ball rolling in preparation for the invasion of England. Philip appointed Álvaro de Bazán, the Marquis of Santa Cruz, to lead the Armada; with an undefeated fifty-year long career, the king was assured that this man would carry out his plans. Santa Cruz asked for 61 first-line ships, but died on the 9th of February 1588 in Lisbon before the ships were fitted out. Philip's replacement for Santa Cruz was Alonso de Guzmán y Sotomayor, 7th Duke of Medina Sidonia, who had little experience in naval warfare – and even less in the leading of men.

The force allocated to Medina-Sidonia numbered 130 ships, 8,000 seamen and 1,900 soldiers with at least 300 in reserve. This enormous fleet also had to be provisioned with food, water, guns and powder.

On the 4th of May 1588 the Armada set sail down the waters of the Tagus. On the 18th of that month, mainsails were shaken out and the fleet commenced its historic yet fateful voyage. Medina's instructions were to sail to Dunkerque in France, where he would meet up with the Duke of Parma who would make available three hundred barges full of soldiers; the Armada would escort these across the English Channel to invade England on the Kent coast. Once landed, the soldiers would then march on London. Parma was a talented soldier and he had managed to mould a hotchpotch of mercenaries into a trained and dangerous fighting force At its core was a division of Spanish infantrymen, soldiers from boyhood for whom fighting was a way of life. Of course, among the soldiers were lots of Gaels, members of a Celtic people for whom war was as attractive as it was to the Spaniards; they had much in common.

In all, Parma had sixty thousand soldiers, of which three thousand were cavalry. Parma's role was to get the invading force onto English soil but he was *not* to attack the English *fleet* unless it was deemed absolutely necessary. Preparations had been carried out in the utmost secrecy and a report was sent to Medina listing every ship in the Armada. The report was circulated in Europe and it was assumed that the Armada would be successful in carrying out its mission. At Greenwich, Walsingham and the Lord Treasurer Burghley had managed to get a copy of the report and they carefully studied the details, unaware that it contained figures that were grossly exaggerated. Elizabeth was kept informed and was involved in deciding how they should respond.

The two things that Philip could not control were the weather, the English Channel being notorious for its currents and sudden changes of wind, and those who commanded the Armada not being experienced sailors.

A Bad Beginning

By the 10th of May, the Armada was concentrated at Belem in Portugal. Santa Cruz had predicted the danger that lay in a late start, but the Armada made slow progress. Sixty-five heavily armed galleons and merchantmen led the line with twenty-five store ships close behind, followed by more than thirty light boats and four galleasses.[2] The unfavourable winds continued to slow the advance and there were signs that some of the food stores were beginning to decay. In the previous December, Elizabeth had ordered the English fleet to be paid off at Chatham,[3] thereby heavily impacting the funds available in the following months. Elizabeth's fleet now only had enough provisions for four weeks, though this could be extended to six weeks by reducing the amount served up.

It was reported to the English that the mighty Armada had been sighted off the English Channel and that it was being affected by bad weather. The Spanish ships slowly sailed up the Channel, yet for a long period of time, there was no sign of the English fleet. Eventually, eleven English ships, commanded by Lord Howard, were finally sighted by the Spanish. Later in the day, the rest of the English ships were also spotted.

There was a limited exchange of fire between the two fleets, but no serious damage to either side. More exchanges continued into the afternoon, with the Armada suffering one serious casualty when

---

2. A hybrid ship that combined the sails and armament of a galleon with the manoeuvrability of the oared galley.

3. *Paid off* means paying the crew onboard all wages earned since the start of the voyage, or since they last received monies. It was also often the point where ships were re-provisioned and the financial accounts balanced.

the *San Salvador* exploded, an accident caused by careless handling of the powder kegs in her magazine. Two galleasses were ordered to take the *San Salvador* in tow, as (it is now believed) she contained a huge fortune in solid gold ducats. The Armada held a particular attraction for the English, as they had been informed that the Spanish ships contained vast amounts of gold.

That evening, the fleets were positioned off Portland and the English attacked – but the Armada sailed on. Neither fleet wanted to fight at close quarters, and soon the Spanish ships reached the Isle of Wight. With some degree of success, the Duke of Medina had completed the first part of his mission. Though there were casualties – around 60 men had been killed in just one day – the Armada was still intact.

Interestingly, the English also considered the situation a success, though they knew that at some point close quarters fighting would be inevitable. On the deck of the English flagship, Lord Howard touched the blade of his sword on the shoulders of two 'sea dogs' – Frobisher and Hawkins – creating them knights, a power that Howard possessed as Lord Admiral of the Fleet.

The Dispersal by Fire

All day the Spanish kept a careful watch on the English fleet astern. Sidonia, Duke of Medina, was expecting an imminent attack. For months, Lord Howard had been working on a battleplan, a strategy of how best to respond to the Spanish threat. That evening, the English held a council of war and, gathered around a table, agreed that it was now time to put that strategy to the test – the decision was said to have been made with great speed.

The English plan was to send in eight fire ships,[4] each manned by one person who would stay aboard until the last minute. This, they hoped, would strike fear within the anchored Armada and cause them to disperse – and thus tipping the odds of battle in their favour.

The plan worked and a battle ensued, during which the Spanish suffered heavy casualties; a number of ships were lost, six hundred men were killed and eight hundred had been wounded. In contrast, the English losses were light – None of their ships had been sunk, and only one hundred men had lost their lives.

There was also a change in the wind, which favoured the English. When morning came, the Spanish ships that were still intact had regrouped and the two fleets were separated by a strip of land. The Spanish were trying to prevent their ships from going aground while the English looked on but could do nothing as they were now almost entirely without powder or shot.

The plight of the Spanish changed once again; this was caused by the weather. They were now forced to sail in a northerly direction, taking them up Britain's east coast. It was thought that they might

---

4. A vessel designed to be set alight and sailed towards the enemy.

be able to take shelter in a Scottish port and possibly even return with the help of the Scots. But the English followed until, with food and water running out, they were forced to take shelter in the Firth of Forth. The fleeing Spanish Armada had no idea of the fate that awaited them as they sailed into the cold grey northern waters.

Panic Stations

Sidonia had failed his royal master and as the fleet sailed north he realised that discipline of the greatest kind would be needed for the ships to be brought back safely to Spain. Sidonia's orders were to have unfortunate results for the captain of the *San Pedro*, which had suffered greatly from English gunshot – it would become the only Armada wreck on the coast of England.

The captain of one of the smaller ships was Francisco de Cuéllar, who later wrote about the progress of the Armada. However, he had enemies at court and was later tried and hanged.

There were also others that wanted to take the matter into their own hands as a result of the failed Armada. There was the crew of the *San Juan de Sicilia* who wanted to head for Norway but in the end didn't, instead following their orders. The men's fate was decided by an explosion on the ship that killed all but fifty men.

The Armada was now situated four hundred miles west of the river Shannon. Dysentery had struck and in nearly every ship the food supplies had started to stink.

For seven weeks the Armada had been at sea; one ship – the *San Martin* – had been badly damaged by the high winds, and other ships were starting to take in water. With 'water everywhere but not a drop to drink', Sidonia decided to head for Ireland. He had with him 110 vessels of the 128 that had started out from Coruña. Some of the Spaniards were familiar with the harbours, and the Irish seas were rich with fish. Repairs to the ships would need to take place prior to sailing back to Spain, but the charts they had were inaccurate. The *San Juan de Portugal* rounded the north coast of Ireland, though some ships were forced onto the shores; those still afloat would head for Sligo and Donegal Bay. The great weight of the guns made the ships difficult to handle in the ensuing gales; one Spanish historian – Fernandez Duro – summed up the reason why Ireland was the graveyard of the Armada: the ships were leaking, they had no anchors, their masts and rigging were in bad shape, and the water casks were smashed. The spring of 1588 had been remarkable for the number, strength and duration of the storms that swept across Europe. Almost from the start, the Armada had been buffeted by strong winds; thunder and lightning had menaced all shipping of all kinds. Those that lived on the edge of the Atlantic were surprised at the rough weather that occurred along the littoral of County Kerry. Even though the Armada failed in its objective, Philip managed to keep his throne.

The Lord Deputy, FitzWilliam

The Lord Deputy of Ireland, Sir William FitzWilliam, was in a panic having failed to carry out Elizabeth's wishes; such a result could end up with him losing his head. There were stories circulating that the Spaniards intended to kill every male child in England, and it was rumoured that within the holds of the Armada, twenty-foot lengths of rope were stored together with large knives for disembowelling... all for the purpose of killing Protestants.

Elizabeth ordered English forces to land in Waterford to combat the Spaniard being forced ashore in Ireland by the high winds. At the same time, many of the Irish in County Kerry were attracted by the rich pickings to be had from the washed-up ships of the Armada.

In an incident in Galway, three hundred Spaniards had gone ashore and been massacred by English troops. The Catholic women of Galway showed their grief by making shrouds for the bodies and all those killed were given a Christian burial. Two of the Spaniards managed to escape and were sheltered by the locals, but would they ever get back to Spain? Executions of Spaniards were commonplace; some were decapitated and very few ever managed to escape.

There was one story of kindness, in which George Bingham, brother of Sir Richard Bingham, gave shelter to some shipwrecked Spaniards, but they were put to the sword when captured on a visit by the Lord Deputy. Captured noblemen were taken from Galway to Athlone and executed.

There were instances when ransoms were demanded and paid; in one such case Luis de Cordova and his nephew were captured, and after a long negotiation, a large ransom was paid to the English and they were returned to Spain.

The names of Spaniards that were executed at Athlone spoke of their nobility and of their unbending military caste. Their fates may be studied through Elizabethan state papers, written in ink that has faded with the passage of time and in a script that makes the modern eye strain; there were no fewer than thirteen Dons. With them died the captain of the *Falco Blanco* and the captain of the *Concepcion*. If one might read between the lines of the State papers, it would appear to suggest that Sir William Bingham intended to put the blame for the executions on the shoulders of FitzWilliam, who claimed that the ships and their men had perished on the shores of Ireland, rather than the crew having being captured and executed.

The Fate of Captain Francisco de Cuéllar

Cuéllar stood at the aft end of his merchantman, the *San Juan de Sicilia*. *La Regazona* was also a large ship of almost 1,300 tons under the command of Don Martín de Bertendona. Less fortunate were those that had sailed on the *San Martinho* – some three hundred men perished on board. Cuéllar did not know the fate of the other ships in the Armada.

For four days Cuéllar's ships had strained at their anchorage on the coast near Benbulben mountain. The ships were driven ashore, but no more than three thousand of the crew escaped, and one thousand men ended up drowning. Cuéllar was fortunate in that he was washed up at a convenient hiding place, where he fell asleep through exhaustion.

Two hundred men were ready to plunder the Spanish gold that was on board the wrecked Spanish galleons, and Cuéllar watched as his fellow countrymen were attacked and put to death. Some of the locals tended the wounds of the Spanish; Cuéllar himself barely survived by eating a meagre diet of herbs. He reached the territory of O'Rourke where he was given shelter and a change of clothes. The chieftain's wife was full of sympathy for the Spaniards, but they were only given one meal a day.

The chieftain MacClancy also sheltered some of the Spanish in his castle. This meant that the English were now intent on marching into MacClancy territory to take up arms with local Gaels who were hostile towards the Spanish. Yet the English found themselves under siege for seventeen days; Cuéllar said that God had "delivered them from the enemy". Cuéllar eventually managed to reach Catholic territory in Scotland where he remained for six months. But it was here that some of the Armada ships had been wrecked, and it is said that he did not enjoy his stay.

During this time, the Duke of Parma was making preparations for his men to return to Spain and vessels were arranged for this purpose. But the returning ships were attacked by the Dutch; two of these ships were captured and all on board were put to death. The other vessels were shipwrecked and most of their crew were drowned. Cuéllar somehow managed to survive once more, swimming ashore in just his shirt.

Some of the Gaels that had helped the Spanish flee to Scotland were arrested. The head of the O'Rourke clan had also fled to Scotland and when found, he was arrested; he would later be hanged in London for high treason.

The chieftain MacClancy also paid dearly for helping the Spanish; he was captured by the English and beheaded, his head taken to Sligo. It was said that he was a barbarous creature and that he was in fact O'Rourke's right-hand man; he had fourteen Spaniards with him when he was captured.

One memento of this great sea drama was an elaborate carved wooden figurehead taken from one of the Armada ships; it came into the possession of Simon Cullen, a rich businessman and Justice of the Peace in Sligo town. Like Cullen however, the figurehead no longer exists. Another remnant of the time was found a little more than a century ago; bones unearthed from the sand dunes of Sligo were believed to have emanated from the 1588 Armada.

A Morbid Interest

In the government papers of the Elizabethan era, there are many statements that can be read with a chill of horror. Recorded in the annals is the fate of many of those lost on the Irish coast. We know that many noblemen were sent to Galway and were among those executed on the orders of the Lord Deputy. There is a also document telling us that a large number of ships were sighted from the coast of County Clare. The *San Marcos* was among the wrecks of that coast, a ship of seven hundred tons and carrying within her wooden hull 264 souls. Just sixty men struggled ashore from the *San Esteban*, leaving in the sea the awful sight of two hundred floating corpses.

Many of the survivors from the Armada were hunted down and hanged, while others died of thirst, hunger or food poisoning. Some of the vessels simply were not built for a journey of this nature, and their crews suffered as a result.

In the northern waters, the ship *Zúñiga* rounded the tip of Ireland and began her way southwards, somehow surviving the gales that caused many other ships to perish. She was sighted off the cliffs of Moher, which rose around seven hundred feet above the sea. *Zúñiga* avoided the worst of the Atlantic waves and the crew were jubilant at their lucky escape, but the ship was letting in water by the time she sailed through the English Channel. For two months she laid up in Le Havre, but her berth silted up and she was abandoned. The surviving Spaniards were severely weakened by afflictions ranging from untended wounds to hunger, thirst and fever. A landing was attempted but the men were so weak that it was easily countered by locally-stationed troops. Things got so desperate that the crew offered Nicholas Cahane, an officer of the Queen, an entire ship –

the carrack *Anunciada* – including guns and powder in exchange for fresh provisions and materials to repair their own vessel. It was a time of desperation. A few days later Cahane must have congratulated himself on having refused the offer, as the ship on offer was stripped of everything that could be moved and was then set on fire. She had been leaking so badly that she could not have stayed afloat much longer. The captain of the *Anunciada* had been Don Pedro de Ivella Ohmuchevich Gargurich, a famous Russian seaman who held the status of an Admiral. The entire ship was burned to the waterline and sank in the Shannon estuary, with the crew taken aboard the *Barc de Zangia* which arrived safely in Spain.

It is likely that the other vessels in whose company the *Barc de Zangia* sailed made a landing on the home Spanish coast; they were fortunate that their pilot was a man who possessed an exact knowledge of both the geography of the Irish coast and the locations of its safe anchorages.

The Noble Company

For almost two weeks the *Rata Santa María Encoronada* had been pitching badly due to the howling winds: there were 419 souls on board, its noblemen know as the "Flower of Spain". The captain of the *Santa María* knew that he needed a safe shelter to mend her sails and rigging. She ran for the Irish coast despite ill winds; although she made some progress windward, most of the Spanish ships were not designed to handle the kind of punishment dealt by the combination of choppy Irish waters and severe weather.

All around the Irish coast were hidden reefs that would challenge even the best of captains, and there were no lighthouses to give seamen any kind of prior warning. And so the Catholic Spaniards put their trust in God. On the nights of the 6th and 7th of August, the *Santa María Encoronada* anchored in Tirraun and Ballycroy respectively, but her anchor dragged and they hit aground at the shore of Ballycroy. The crew set their beached ship on fire, and with a headcount numbering that of a small army, these men – under the command of Don Alonso de Guzmán y Sotomayor – were able to overrun some of the local Gaelic castles in the region of County Mayo.

Today, there are many stories of Spanish gold waiting to be discovered around the coast of Ireland. Onboard the ships were many nobles who travelled with fine plate, gold, silver, coin and jewels. Don Alonso himself was of such high status that he had no fewer than thirty-six servants at his bidding.

Don Alonso's men soon met up with two ships: the *Duquesa Santa Ana* (from which Alonso ran his command) and the *Nuestra Señora de Begoña*; these vessels had brought in over six hundred men between them. Yet bad luck dogged the Spanish and in addition to this, they were now vastly overcrowded, with more than eight hundred souls aboard the lead ship.

The *Santa Ana* made for Donegal Bay but was blown against the rocks and became wrecked at Loughros – though all aboard managed to make it ashore. These men were fully armed and intent on obtaining provisions in County Mayo, and as things stood they would certainly be a match for the English. Luck was not on the side of Don Alonso, however. He had damaged his leg when the ship had floundered, and had to be carried in a litter, still in much pain after a resting period of nine days had not seen him heal. He ordered his men to head for Killybegs, where three Spanish ships had been forced into the bay. One of these vessels was the *Girona*, which had a smashed rudder; the others were leaking badly and in need of serious repairs, having been battered and mauled by the wind and waves. Low on provisions, the Spanish were given shelter by the MacSweeney clan.

After two weeks spent repairing the *Girona*, she was ready to set sail and brave the Atlantic swell. She sailed past Lough Swilly and Lough Foyle, setting her sights on Scotland.

Sailing with well over a thousand men on board, tragedy struck the *Girona* as she approached Lacada Point in County Antrim. Vast waves had once again smashed the ship's rudder, and she was wrecked against what are now called the Spanish Rocks. Over the course of an hour, all but nine men would lose their lives, wiping out a significant section of Spanish nobility.

Around 260 were washed ashore, buried by the locals amongst the great petrified lava mass of the Giants Causeway. The remainder were swallowed by the sea to find a resting place that has never been marked.

A Broken Pledge

Lord Treasurer Burghley broke the seal of a letter that had arrived from Ireland and found that its contents recorded the fate of the Spaniards massacred on board *La Trinidad Valencera*, a great ship of over one thousand tons and armed with forty-two guns, that had sailed from Coruña with 360 men on board.

By the time the vessel neared the coast of Donegal, she was letting in water; the captain decided to lay anchor in Glenagivney Bay. The ship was under the command of the Duke of Tuscany and was part of the Armada. The *Trinidad Valencera* had in fact previously taken on 264 men from the floundering *Barca de Amburgo*, a transport ship of some six hundred tons that had become swamped by the heavy seas. In Glenagivney Bay however, *La Trinidad Valencera* began listing to such a degree that the order was given to abandon ship.

The Spaniards paid 200 ducats to the Gaels, who supplied them with clothing along with a small boat in which men were ferried ashore from the slowly-sinking *Trinidad*, a process that took two days. Under the command of Don Alonso, the Spanish attempted a seven-day march inland, but were found by the Hovendens, foster brothers of the 3rd Earl of Tyrone.

The Spanish laid down their arms and agreed to surrender. With the guarantee of safe conduct into the hands of the Lord Deputy FitzWilliam given, the noblemen, ship's captain and military leaders – including Don Alonso – were separated from the rank and file. On the following night however, the defenceless Spaniards were massacred without mercy. Some three hundred men were killed and the grass became flooded and soaked with blood. It was a dark period in Irish history; now it is said ghosts walk the land and cry out in despair.

A mere 159 men escaped by running blindly through the furze and marsh. Some were sheltered by Sorley Boy MacDonnell, a man who was no friend of the English. Four hundred of his people – a garrison of troops and a number of civilian women and children – had been massacred by the Queen's men under the command of John Norris and Francis Drake; many who initially escaped their fate had been hunted down and killed. Others found shelter with the MacSweeneys in Doe Castle.

The treachery with which Richard and Henry Hovenden dealt with their captors was hidden by them in reports to the Lord Deputy. Their claim was that they had come across five Spaniards in a village called Elliagh and had sent an emissary to report on the situation for Elizabeth. They wrote that the Spanish had intended to invade England – for Ireland was England's back door – but had been forced to land here due to bad weather. According to the Hovendens, by nightfall six hundred Spanish men had set up camp and at around midnight, skirmishes had broken out resulting in the deaths of around two hundred men.

Those from the rank and file who escaped the bloodshed ended up at the house of bishop of Derry Redmond O'Gallagher, and were sent to Scotland, before eventually being returned to Spain. The forty-five nobles and officers who had been initially separated from their men were marched to Dublin, but only two thirds of them survived the ordeal. These thirty were taken to London for ransom back to King Philip.

Death at the Blasket Islands

From the north-west, the galleon *San Juan de Portugal* was under the command of Juan Martínez de Recalde – a knight of the order of Santiago – and was attempting to approach the shore. She was a large ship, displacing over one thousand tons, carrying five hundred men and with the firepower of twenty heavy cannons. Alongside the *San Juan* were a smaller 750-ton Spanish vessel and a ship captured from the Scots. Landfall was sighted; it was the great towering bulk of Mount Brandon that dominated Dingle Bay and was normally covered in a blanket of cloud.

But as the ships approached the Blasket Islands off the coast of Kerry, they were intercepted by the English. Recalde, a native of Bilbao, had been commanding Spanish ships for sixteen years, but it was here that he met his end. The *San Juan de Portugal* was in the thick of the fighting, firing powerful broadsides at the largest of the enemy vessels, but he was killed as the English returned fire.

On the 2nd of September, the *San Juan Bautista* had – according to its paymaster, Marcos de Aramburu – been floundering off the coast, with no one on board certain of their position. All they had sight of were great white waves and sunken reefs, and when the wind began to freshen they were soon taking in water. Below deck many were crushed on account of the sheer number of men sheltering from the fierce weather. By five in the morning, the *Bautista* began to shudder heavily in the wind, which de Aramburu wrote was blowing with "great force". When dawn broke, her lookouts scanned the horizon for the sight of mastheads but to no avail, such was the strength of the storm. Fortune then smiled on de Aramburu; he finally sighted two vessels that had been companions to the *Bautista* during the night. The problem for the Spanish was that they had no charts of the waters around Blasket Islands that were accurate enough for safe navigation. Approaching Great Blasket Island was enough to frighten any sailor, with its four-mile-long passage that spanned just half a mile wide, surrounded by ridges nearly six hundred feet high.

Although destruction seemed almost inevitable for the ships, the *San Juan de Portugal* successfully managed to negotiate the passage into the sound, and the *San Juan Bautista* followed in its wake, along with a captured Scottish fishing vessel.

Small parties went ashore, where some succeeded in obtaining fresh water and provisions. However, eight men were captured; among them was a Scot. They were suffering from sickness and were clearly undernourished from a lack of victuals. It was also clear that they had a complete lack of knowledge regarding the area in which they had dropped anchor. Three more Spanish ships joined those in the sound, but two sank – the *Santa Maria de la Rosa* and the *San Juan de Ragusa*. All the Spanish ships were by now in terrible condition; De Aramburu reported that the *San Martinez* had been taking in water for three days, and the *San Juan de Portugal* had actually collided with the *Bautista*.

The small 75-ton *Nuestra Señora del Socorro* had made for the straits, but anchored at Fenit on the Irish mainland. Three of the crew volunteered to swim ashore to seek water and provisions. They were captured by officers of the crown, and the entire desperate, hungry crew surrendered. They were marched to Tralee castle, the seat of Sir Edward and Lady Margaret Denny. Passing under the portcullis, flares cast an eerie light on the flagged floor and rough plastered walls. With Sir Edward not present, the men were presented to Lady Denny who made a dreadful order: All twenty-four men should be hanged, as there was no prison large enough to hold them all.

Three Irish locals pleaded that they had friends in Waterford who would ransom the captured men, but such pleas went unheeded. A gibbet was erected at the Market Cross in Tralee, and the twenty-four men were hanged in a barbaric fashion: by slow strangulation (rather than the 'quick drop' that would break the neck and result in an instant – rather than painful and drawn out – death).

The next day, Sir Edward returned from Dublin where he attended a meeting of the council. There, he was told the information that had been gleaned from the prisoners: the great ships of the Armada had anchored at the Blaskets. This news frightened Sir Edward, who was unaware of the poor condition of the ships and their men; he believed a landing of the Spanish force would bring about a terrible retribution.

Graveyard of a Prince

Sir Edward Denny was a typical Englishman and had come to Ireland in the reign of Elizabeth during the plantation; he is known to have remarked that Ireland was a country steeped in the past. Those that accompanied him from England were known as 'undertakers', they were assigned plots of land that had been confiscated from the Irish Earl of Desmond. These plots varied in size from four thousand to twelve thousand acres, each of which would be allocated to a 'planter', of which there were hundreds, who would also be given the sum of £278 for seed, stock and food – plenty sufficient for the first year of their occupation. Sir Edward had been given the grant of Tralee Castle. The English had hoped that the Irish colony would absorb thousands of peasantry that roamed the English countryside.

While the Spanish ships lay in the sound at the Blasket Islands, the forces of Elizabeth assembled at Dingle to meet the great invasion of the Spanish that they expected to happen at any moment.

Amongst the yellowed pages of the archives of England are documents which provide an insight to the fates of those who sailed from Spain with the Armada; many tales – both true and false – were told under interrogation. One such story was told by the lone survivor of the *Santa Maria de la Rosa*, which had sunk quickly after entering the sound. He asserted that the Prince of Ascoli, son of the King of Spain himself, had gone down with the ship. Near the schoolhouse at Dunquin[5] is a spot which became known for centuries as *Uaig Mhic Ri na Spainne* – the graveyard of the King of Spain.

---

5. A town on mainland Ireland near Blasket Sound

One David Gwynne, a Welsh galley slave, told an heroic tale of how he had freed his fellow slaves. He claimed that he had captured one of the ships and brought them all to a French port. However, the ship he claimed to have sailed to France was, of course, the *Santa Maria de la Rosa*, whose only survivor – Antonia de Monana – was executed at Dingle.

On the day that de Monana was put to death, Marcos de Aramburu faced the tide and had attempted to flee the sound with the *San Juan Bautista* via the southern entrance. He failed in his efforts however, and next tried to exit through the north-west passage among the reefs. At first things looked promising, but soon great clouds passed across the waters, and the ship's crew knew they would have a storm to contend with. After a three-hour-long pounding by the storm, the wind changed, veering to the west. All the *Bautista* could do was wait until morning; she had been stripped of her sails by the storm.

When dawn broke, to their utter dismay, the *Bautista* crew found themselves back at the opening of the Blasket Sound from which they had made their escape. Incredibly, the ship endured a great gale; the Spaniards were great seamen and managed to bring the dangerous conditions under control. Finally, the crew having repaired as much of the ship as they could, de Aramburu successfully set sail for home.

Three days later, the rest of the ships anchored in the sound began the voyage home, following Juan Martínez de Recalde on the *San Juan de Portugal*. Juan Martinez was a courageous sailor, but did not survive for long after his arrival back in Spain; illness – most likely caused by malnutrition and other health issues on the unsuccessful voyage – let to his death less than one month after making it home.

The centuries roll on and the sea still rushes through the Blaskets. Only eighty years ago, a fisherman dragged up a small brass cannon that had a coat of arms engraved on the barrel; this was all of the Armada given up by the seas of the Count Kerry coast.

The village of Tralee grew into a town and the Denny's castle fell into ruin. As the years passed, the stones of the castle were pulled down to make a roadway; the road today is a street in Tralee, with the appropriate name of *Denny Street*.

Afterword

The main part of the Armada had sailed far into the Atlantic and Alonso de Guzmán y Sotomayor, 7th Duke of Medina Sidonia, now commanded sixty ships which all rounded Cape Clear on the southern tip of Ireland. Only now did the gales cease.

After a comparatively uneventful voyage, the Duke sighted Coruña, but his crew on the *San Martin* were weakened and could not immediately make their way into the harbour.

Day by day the ships made their way to Biscay ports, but for the sick – of which there were huge numbers – hospital beds were few, and both food and water was scarce. Some even died of the plague.

Juan Martinez de Recalde was now dead, along with many other commanders. According to a merchant called William Herbert, who reported the plight of the crews to the Spanish crown, the Duke of Medina Sidonia was so disabled that having come ashore, a week passed before he could be removed on a litter and transported to his home at San Lucar. The King forbade Medina Sidonia to approach within seven leagues of his court, though the Duke continued to serve his master well as governor of Cadiz.

However, an Irish merchant by the name of Edward Walsh reported a different story to the council at Waterford. He described how the Duke remained on board his ship for seven days before being carried ashore, followed by fifty-nine gentlemen in mourning.

And so ended the tragic fate of the Spanish Armada. The Atlantic, in which so many lives were lost in 1588, still breaks upon the shores where the Armada was wrecked.

Printed in Great Britain
by Amazon

33925034R00030